# PARENTS & CHILDREN

## God's Design for the Family

### BOOK 2

NAVPRESS
A MINISTRY OF THE NAVIGATORS
P.O. Box 20, Colorado Springs, Colorado 80901

The Navigators is an international, evangelical Christian organization. Jesus Christ gave His followers the Great Commission to go and make disciples (Matthew 28:19). The aim of The Navigators is to help fulfill that commission by multiplying laborers for Christ in every nation.

NavPress is the publishing ministry of The Navigators. NavPress publications are tools to help Christians grow. Although publications alone cannot make disciples or change lives, they can help believers learn biblical discipleship, and apply what they learn to their lives and ministries.

Scripture quotations are from the *New International Version,* © 1978 by the New York International Bible Society.

Printed in the United States of America

# CONTENTS

# IN RECOGNITION

These staff members of The Navigators made the major contribution to the prayerful and thoughtful preparation of *God's Design for the Family*: Rod Beidler, Bruce Das, Ray Hoo, Doug Prensner, Ed Reis, Gene Soderberg, and Bob Sparks. The aim of the series has been to provide married couples with biblical principles and patterns that lead to dynamic family growth in love, and to harmony in their relationships with God and their families.

In addition, appreciation is due to the wives of the staff members, who provided help and ideas as the project developed; to other Navigator staff members who participated in various stages of planning and preparing the series; and to a large number of staff, pastors, and lay men and women who field-tested the manuscripts.

# BEFORE YOU BEGIN

These studies are written for use by married couples, or by singles planning to be married. Both partners should answer the questions separately and then discuss them with each other. You will gain even more benefit by meeting regularly with other couples after all of you have answered the questions. The recommended pace is one chapter per week, with a group discussion time for each chapter. Group discussion guidelines for all the chapters are included in this book, beginning on page 83.

Each chapter includes application questions and suggested family project ideas to help you apply to your family life the things you are learning in your study. Before deciding on each application, remember to pray about it. God knows the needs in your life which He wants you to work on now. Stay in communication with Him as you plan, and be confident that He will lead you. Pray also for insight and strength in putting your applications into practice.

## CHAPTER 1

# GOALS FOR PARENTS

RAISING children is a God-given privilege and requires thorough preparation as well as commitment. Successfully building a God-fearing family requires patience, diligence, and an understanding of some foundational biblical principles.

## CHILDREN ARE A GIFT FROM GOD

1. Read Psalm 127:3-5, and summarize what this passage says about children.

   _____

   _____

   _____

   _____

   _____

2. What view of children (or grandchildren) is given in these passages?

   Genesis 33:4-5_____

   _____

   _____

Proverbs 17:6 _____

_____

_____

Matthew 19:14 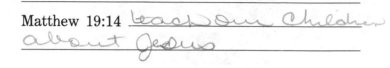 teach our children about Jesus

_____

3. Hannah, the mother of Samuel, had been childless for many years before his birth. Read her prayer in 1 Samuel 1:10-11, God's answer to the prayer (1:19-20), and Hannah's response to His answer (1:27-28). How would you describe Hannah's attitude toward children?

_____

_____

_____

_____

_____

_____

_____

_____

_____

_____

_____

## THE RESPONSIBILITY OF PARENTS

4. What responsibilities are assigned to fathers in Ephesians 6:4 and Colossians 3:21?

10

_____

_____

_____

_____

_____

_____

How would you explain these responsibilities in
your own words?

_____

_____

_____

_____

_____

_____

_____

_____

How can a wife help her husband in fulfilling
these responsibilities?

_____

_____

_____

_____

_____

_____

_____

5. Although a man's responsibility for his children's instruction is clear, the primary command given to him regarding his family is to love his wife, as indicated in Ephesians 5:25, Colossians 3:19, and 1 Peter 3:7. Read each of these passages. If a husband practices these principles, what effect do you think it would have on his children?

_____

_____

_____

_____

_____

_____

_____

_____

What effect do you think it would have if they are *not* practiced?

insecurity

6. In Titus 2:4-5, Paul gave guidelines for training young women in their responsibilities to their families. List these guidelines, and tell why you think it is important for a mother to practice them.

_____

_____

_____

_____

_____

_____

_____

_____

_____

_____

_____

_____

7. Read Deuteronomy 6:1-9. This passage includes commands Moses received from God to pass on to the people of Israel. Why did God give these commands? (verse 2)

_____

_____

_____

_____

How were these truths to be passed on to their children? (verses 6-9)

_____

_____

_____

_____

_____

Describe in your own words the kind of relationships the parents were to have with God. (verse 5)

_____

_____

_____

_____

_____

_____

Why do you think it was important for the parents to have these commands upon their hearts? (verse 6)

_____

_____

_____

_____

_____

_____

8. Look again at Deuteronomy 6:7. What are some of the best "teachable moments" you can use in your family to teach your children God's commandments?

_____

_____

_____

_____

_____

_____

9. Read God's purpose for choosing Abraham in Genesis 18:18-19. What was Abraham's responsibility toward his children?

_____

_____

_____

_____

10. Explain how the principles you observe in the passages below can be applied to your responsibility as a parent.

2 Corinthians 12:14-15_____

_____

_____

_____

1 Timothy 5:8_____

_____

_____

_____

## A PROMISE FOR PARENTS

11. God gives a conditional promise to parents in Proverbs 22:6—"Train a child in the way he should go, and when he is old he will not turn from it." In the *Modern Language Bible*\* (Berkeley version) this verse is "Educate a child according to his life requirements; even when he is old he will not veer from it." Paraphrase this verse in your own words on the next page.

\**Modern Language Bible,* © 1969 by the Zondervan Publishing House, Grand Rapids, Michigan.

_____

_____

_____

_____

_____

_____

_____

_____

_____

_____

Three important concepts can be identified from this verse:

(1) Training is an essential process in raising children.

(2) Parents should have standards and purpose in training children: They should teach each child "in the way he should go."

(3) Proper training is not in vain, but brings about a definite result when the child reaches adulthood.

## SEEING OUR CHILDREN MATURE

12. Read Luke 2:52. In what four areas did Jesus grow as a child?

_____

_____

_____

Using these four areas as categories, make a list below of some attitudes and abilities you would like your children to have by the time they are ready to leave your family and become independent. These would be qualities or abilities you feel they will need in order to become the persons God intends them to be. You may want to make separate lists in some areas for sons and daughters, or perhaps a separate list for each child.

*Mental*—In this area you could include mental abilities and attitudes. You might want to list educational accomplishments as well.

_____

_____

_____

_____

_____

_____

_____

*Physical*—What will your children need to know about their bodies in order to properly treat them as temples of the Holy Spirit?

_____

_____

_____

_____

_____

_____

_____

*Spiritual*—What will your children need to know, experience, be, and do to grow spiritually? What should characterize their relationship with God?

_____

_____

_____

_____

_____

_____

*Social*—How will they need to relate to others—Christians and non-Christians?

_____

_____

_____

_____

_____

_____

Once you and your spouse have completed your lists, plan a time to discuss and combine them. Then pray together for each child according to what you have written.

## APPLICATION

(In the application section at the end of each chapter you may find it helpful to discuss what you have written with your spouse, and perhaps with others in the family.)

13. Prayerfully review your answers in this chapter. Summarize on the next page the principles you studied which most impressed you.

_____

_____

_____

_____

_____

_____

_____

_____

_____

14. List any need in your life relating to your responsibility as a parent which you believe you should
work on at this time.

_____

_____

_____

What passage of Scripture in this chapter relates
to this need?

_____

_____

_____

What specific action will you take?

_____

_____

_____

_____

How will you evaluate your progress?

_____

_____

## SUGGESTED
## FAMILY
## PROJECT

(This project, and those listed at the end of later
chapters, can be a valuable exercise for practicing
the scriptural principles you have studied in this
chapter. As you read the instructions for the projects, think of creative ways to make them meaningful
and enjoyable for each member of your family. Plan
to include every child who is old enough to enjoy the
time with you. If your children are older, allow time
for deeper discussion of thoughts and questions they
may have, and let them help you plan the project.)

Read together Luke 2:41-52, and talk specifically
about the four areas of growth mentioned in the last
verse. Mention some way you have observed each
child mature in the four areas recently. Then have
each of them talk about a specific way he would like
to continue growing in one or more of these areas.
You may want to discuss with your children how
they can begin working on these goals.

CHAPTER 2

# INSTRUCTIONS FOR CHILDREN

JUST as He does for parents, God provides specific instructions in the Scriptures for children. Parents need to know these, and help their children understand and obey them.

## HONORING FATHER AND MOTHER

1. Read Deuteronomy 5:16, the fifth of the Ten Commandments. List everything you think the word *honor* means in this verse.

   *Respect your parents do what they say*

   What observations did Paul make about this commandment in Ephesians 6:1-3?

   *Obey + honor your parents because God placed them in authority if you honor them you will have a long life full of blessing*

21

The child is instructed in this commandment to honor both father and mother. What does this imply to you?

*That God placed both parents over the child, that they should be united*

2. Read Luke 2:41-51. As a child, how did Jesus follow the fifth commandment?

*He returned home + was obedient to his parent*

3. From these passages, tell how Jesus expressed obedience and honor to His heavenly Father:

John 4:31-34 *he expressed his food was to obey the will of the one who sent him to finish the work he was sent to do*

John 5:30 *he passed no judgment without consulting the Father.*

John 6:37-40 *That he had come from heaven to do the will of God, who sent him, not his own*

John 17:4 *he brought glory to God on earth by doing everything he was told to do*

4. Read Mark 7:9-13. From this passage, what observation can you make about Jesus' view of the commandments He quoted?

*He considered them laws from God that they should be obeyed*

## HELPING CHILDREN LEARN OBEDIENCE

5. Read Colossians 3:20. What reason did Paul give here for children to obey their parents?

*Because it pleases the Lord*

How do you think parents can best communicate this reason for obedience to children?

*by telling them children are obedient to their parents + parents are obedient to God*

6. Look again at Ephesians 6:1-3. What could you expect to happen if a child does not honor and obey his parents?

*that he would not have a long life full of blessings*

7. What promise is given in Proverbs 14:26?

*that reverence for God gives man strength + his children a place of refuge + security*

Why do you think this is true?

*Because the say so*

_____

8. Review the instructions for a father's responsibility in Ephesians 6:4 and Colossians 3:21. How will a father's obedience to these commands help his children to obey him?

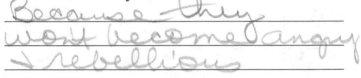

*Because they wont become angry + rebellious*

9. Review the instructions for a mother's responsibility in Titus 2:4. How will a mother's application of this verse help her children to obey her?

*By setting a good example*

_____

It has been said that we should address our children positively three times for every time we speak negatively to them. Does your child get your attention only when he does wrong, or do you express praise and appreciation when he does well (for example, when he plays happily alone or demonstrates initiative)?

10. Read 1 Samuel 3:11-14 and 4:14-17. How did God deal with Eli's sons?

*He punished them for their disobedience*

Read Jeremiah 35:1-10 and 18-19. How did God deal with Jonadab's sons?

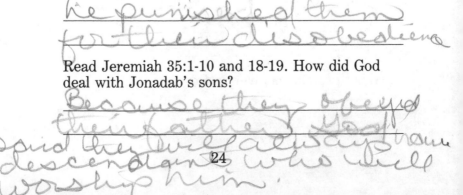

*Because they obeyed their father God said they will always have descendants who will worship him.*

How would you explain the difference?

_Eli's sons disobeyed him + encured God's wrath, Jonadale's sons incured God's favor_

11. Disobedience to parents is included in a list of sins in Romans 1:28-32. Read this passage, and summarize your observations about the source and severity of this sin.

_They had given up God + would not acknowledge him. Severe-listed with hateful minate_

12. Learning to obey his parents can help influence a child to obey God, and to respect and obey other authorities as well. What forms of obedience are commanded in these verses?

Romans 13:1 _Obey the government_

Hebrews 13:17 _Obey your spiritual leaders_

What practical things could you do to help your children understand their responsibilities in these areas?

_By showing good examples_

## INGREDIENTS
## FOR GROWTH

We depend on God's help to build character and proper attitudes in our children. We express this dependence on God through prayer, and by helping our children learn to understand His Word on their own.

13. Read 1 Chronicles 29:1. What did David say about his son Solomon and the task before him?

_that he was young + inex perienced + the work ahead of him is enormous_

What did he pray, therefore, for Solomon? (1 Chronicles 29:19)

_God, for a good heart toward God, + that he would want to obey God in the smallest details + do it eagerly_

Make a list of things to pray for each of your children this week.

_1. that they obey God
2. know right from wrong_

14. Read 2 Timothy 1:5 and 3:14-15. What can you observe about Timothy's childhood from these verses?

26

_That he was raised knowing the scriptures by people faithful to God_

How would you evaluate your children's knowledge of the Scriptures?

_not to good yet but theire learning_

In His actions toward us, God—who is our heavenly Father—shows us how to care for our own children. He loves, teaches, guides, and provides for us. He accepts us as we are, and loves us faithfully even when we disappoint Him or get into trouble. He understands us, rewards us, and disciplines us fairly for our good. Through His love, we see how important we are to Him.

In the same way, we can communicate to our children how important they are—both to God and to us. This will help them develop a healthy sense of personal dignity and self-worth.

15. Study the following passages to find truths relating to our worth to God, and rewrite them in your own words as if you were explaining these truths to your children.

27

Genesis 1:26-27 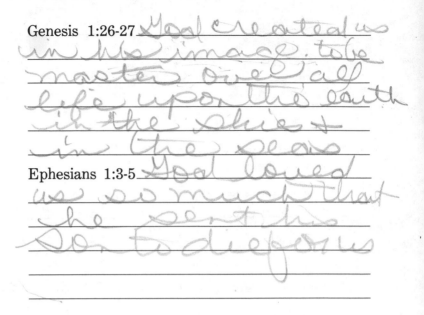 God created us in his image. to be master over all life upon the earth in the skies + in the seas

Ephesians 1:3-5 God loved us so much that he sent his Son to die for us

## APPLICATION

16. Prayerfully review your answers in this chapter, then make a list of the most important things you believe you should provide for your children.

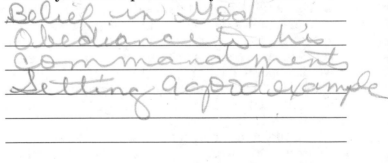 Belief in God Obediance to his commandments Setting a good example

17. Do you believe your children have a sufficient understanding of their responsibility to obey their parents? If not, write down what you believe you and your spouse should do to help them understand their responsibility.

28

*I think they do.*

18. List any need in your life relating to your responsibility as a parent which you believe you should work on at this time.

*Setting a better example*

What passage of Scripture in this chapter relates to this need?

*Titus 2:4*

What specific action will you take?

*Be more consistent in discipline*

How will you evaluate your progress?

*By the kid's action*

## SUGGESTED
## FAMILY
## PROJECT

Read together with your spouse Psalm 78:1-8, then discuss especially verses 4-8. Find examples of your responsibility as parents, as well as your children's responsibility. Then pray together about these.

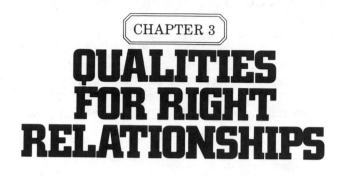

CHAPTER 3

# QUALITIES FOR RIGHT RELATIONSHIPS

GROWING together and learning from each other requires certain attitudes and relationships on the part of each family member. Maintaining these right attitudes is a continual task, and needs frequent evaluation.

## LOVE AND ACCEPTANCE

1. Read Hebrews 5:1-2. Why were the high priests able to deal gently with sinners?

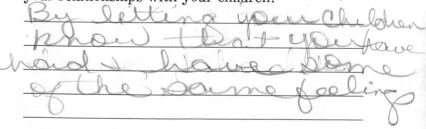

*Because they were men, + were surrounded with the same temptation*

How do you think this example can be applied to your relationships with your children?

*By letting your children know that you have had + have some of the same feeling*

2. List the qualities of love mentioned in 1 Corinthians 13:4-7.

_patient, kind never_
_jealous or envious_
_boastful or proud_
_never haughty_
_selfish or rude love_
_does not demand its_
_own way It is not_
_irritable or touchy_
_Does not hold a grudge &_
_knows when others do wrong_
_never glad about injustice_
_loyal no matter what the cost_
_help you_

Give an example of how someone in your family has recently demonstrated one of these qualities.

_expect the best & defend him_

_Kevin dropped cases on_
_the floor spilling_
_the powder — Donald_
_was patient &_
_understanding_

In your own life, which of these qualities are the most difficult for you to maintain in your relationships with others in your family?

_Being patient_

3. What quality of Christian maturity is mentioned in Ephesians 4:15?

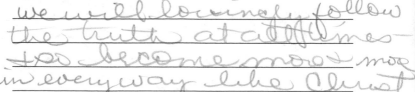

*We will lovingly follow the truth at all times to become more and more in every way like Christ*

How could the other members of your family be affected if you speak the truth to them without love?

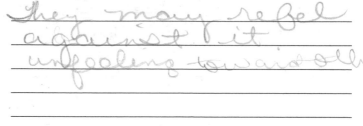

*They may rebel against it unfeeling toward others*

4. In raising children, parents need to learn a proper balance in various aspects of their leadership style, such as those listed below. For each of these pairs of leadership traits, evaluate your own style of leading as a parent, and tell whether you believe you have a proper balance in that area. (The proper balance may vary for different children.)

Providing authority/Allowing proper freedom

Evaluation: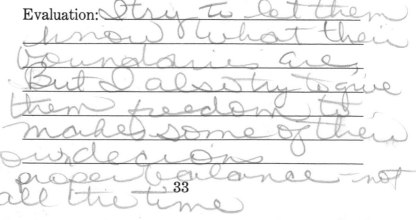

*I try to let them know what their boundaries are, But I also try to give them freedom to make some of their own decisions — proper balance — not all the time*

Providing correction and discipline/Giving encouragement and showing acceptance

Evaluation: _when I correct them_
_etc + let know what_
_it isabout their_
_behaviour that I'm_
_upset with. I let_
_them know its their_
_behaviour, not them I'm_
_upset with_

Providing personal guidance/Allowing for growth in responsibility and initiative

Evaluation: _Sometime_
_too busy o preoccupied_
_to give guidance_

What modifications, if any, do you believe you should make in your style of leadership?

_Being more_
_constant_

34

5. From these statements to the Thessalonians, tell what parental principles Paul applied in training his spiritual children.

1 Thessalonians 2:7 _gentle with them as a mother_

1 Thessalonians 2:10-12 _pure, honest faultless talked to you as a father to his own children pleading, encouraging + even understanding_

## LEARNING FROM AN OLD TESTAMENT FAMILY

In this section you will study the account in Genesis of Isaac's family.

6. Read Genesis 25:19-28. How did Isaac and Rebekah differ in their attitudes toward their sons?

_Esau was owned by Isaac because he was a hunter + Jacob by Rebekah because he was quiet_

What do you think caused this difference in attitudes?

_Difference in interests parent were divided_

35

7. From Genesis 25:24-34, list all the contrasts you observe between Esau and Jacob.

| ESAU | JACOB |
| --- | --- |
| skillful hunter | liked to stay home |
| older | younger |
| favored by father | favored by mother |
| doer | thinker |

From the evidence in this passage, how would you describe the relationship between the two brothers?

_Rivalry_

8. If your family includes two or more children, briefly list the major ways in which they differ in personality.

_Kevin is more outgoing talkative also sensitive — Brian is quiet & stubborn_

36

_____
_____
_____
_____
_____
_____
_____
_____
_____
_____

9. Read Genesis 27:1-41. How did Rebekah demonstrate her favoritism for Jacob?

By helping him trick Isaac into giving him the blessing he would have given Esau

How did Jacob respond to his mother's attitude?

He felt that Isaac would curse him but he let his mother talk him into it

37

Summarize Esau's reaction to the deceit practiced by Rebekah and Jacob.

_He was very angry & wanted to kill Jacob_

10. Read Genesis 27:42—28:5. What attitude toward Jacob did Isaac and Rebekah demonstrate in this passage?

_favoritism by both Isaac & Rebekah_

11. Given their sons' differences, how do you think Isaac and Rebekah could have prevented the antagonism that developed between Jacob and Esau?

_By recognizing that they both were individuals + accepting them as they were. not showing obvious favoritism_

38

12. What need do you see in your family for greater
love and unity?

*more love + understanding*
*Bible Study*

_____

_____

_____

_____

_____

Give a specific example where this need was
recently made evident.

_____

_____

_____

_____

_____

What can you do to meet this need?

_____

_____

_____

_____

_____

## DEVELOPING A LEARNER'S ATTITUDE

A child's life will be greatly enriched the more open
he is to guidance and instruction. A learner's attitude

39

is one of the primary marks of a disciple of Jesus
Christ—one we all must maintain whatever our age.

13. Read Proverbs 1:7. What is the key to growing in
    knowledge?

    *To trust & be
    reverent to the Lord*

14. Summarize briefly the teachings about wisdom in
    Proverbs 1:20-33.

    *Warning of the
    neglect of wisdom
    & choose not to
    trust & reverence
    the Lord*

15. Read Proverbs 2:1-6. Who is the source of
    wisdom?

    *the Lord*

    What attitudes and actions allow us to know God?

    *Listening & Obeying
    & Trusting & being
    reverent to the
    Lord*

16. The theme of Proverbs 8 is an appeal made by wisdom. What principles for gaining wisdom are taught in verses 17 and 34?

*To love the Lord peach you will find*

*you want to be with the Lord that you are waiting*

17. What method of learning is illustrated in Proverbs 24:30-34?

*Observation?*

18. How does Proverbs 19:20 stress the value of having a learner's attitude?

*Get all the advice you can & be wise the rest of you life*

19. Read Proverbs 10:1. How will a child's relationship with his parents be enhanced by his learning wisdom?

*Father & mother will be happy*

41

20. What do you believe are the most important ways you can help your children develop a desire for wisdom?

_By urging them to try for more + By example, teaching them the Bible_

## APPLICATION

21. Prayerfully review your answers in this chapter. List here the things you learned which are most meaningful to you.

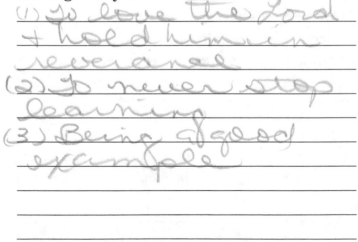

_(1) To love the Lord + hold him in reverance (2) To never stop learning (3) Being a good example_

22. Related to what you learned in this chapter, list any need in your family or your own life that you believe you should work on at this time.

*Being a good example
Remberiing that kids
are observing.*

What passage of Scripture in this chapter relates
to this need?

What specific action will you take?

How will you evaluate your progress?

## SUGGESTED FAMILY PROJECT

Have each family member make a list of practical ex-
pressions of love which he could show to another
family member this week. Don't share your lists with
each other—instead, surprise one another with these
unexpected tokens of love.

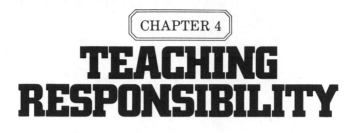

# CHAPTER 4
# TEACHING RESPONSIBILITY

EVERY child is created in God's image, and has personal abilities and unique responsibilities given him by God. To reach their potential, children must be taught how to appropriate God's wisdom and grace to make right decisions.

## SOWING AND REAPING

1. What truths about sowing and reaping do you observe in Galatians 6:7-9?

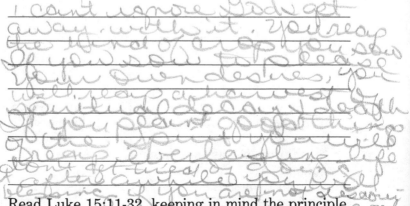

2. Read Luke 15:11-32, keeping in mind the principle of reaping what we sow. What lessons do you

think the younger son learned from his experience
in the distant country?

*Spent all his wealth & wished he had it. He learned how much his father loved him.*

3. What concepts of responsibility did Jesus teach in
Luke 16:10-12?

*To be honest in all matters small or large. If you are not trustworthy with your wealth on earth who will trust you with the riches of heaven. If you are faithful with other's why should you be entrusted with your own*

4. In the process of growth, God promises many
blessings to those who follow His principles and
commands. Our children will richly benefit from
these promises as they learn to follow God's
guidelines.

From Proverbs 3:1-12, list the things we are
commanded to do or not to do, and what is promised if we obey.

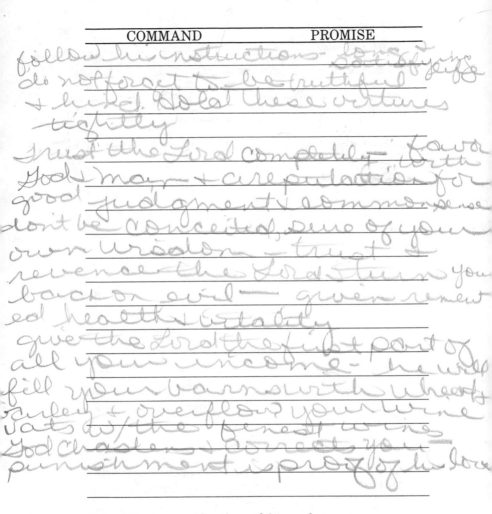

| COMMAND | PROMISE |
|---|---|
| follow his instructions — *[satisfying?]* life | |
| do not forget to be truthful & kind. Hold these virtues tightly | |
| trust the Lord completely — | favor with |
| God & man. + a reputation for | |
| good judgment & common sense | |
| don't be conceited, sure of your | |
| own wisdom — trust | |
| reverence the Lord. Turn you | |
| back on evil — | given renew ed health & vitality |
| give the Lord the first part of all your income — | he will fill your barns with wheat & overflow your wine vats w/ the finest wines |
| God chastens & corrects you — | punishment is proof of his love |

Set aside a specific time this week to pray together with your spouse, asking God to develop these qualities in your children.

5. Take one concept from Proverbs 3:1-12, and plan with your spouse an exercise (such as a short lesson for your family devotional time) to help your children understand the concept. Write out your plan on the next page.

*Proverbs 3 -*
*Read 11-12 aloud +*
*explain like the*
*Lord does that*
*if you didn't love*
*them you wouldn't*
*descipline them*

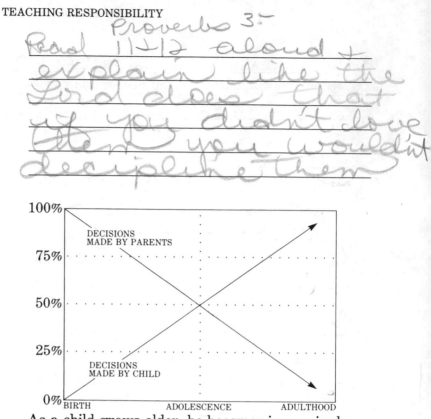

As a child grows older, he becomes increasingly responsible for making decisions about all aspects of his life.

6. Read Jesus' parable of the unmerciful servant in Matthew 18:21-35. What can you learn from this passage about being a model for your children?

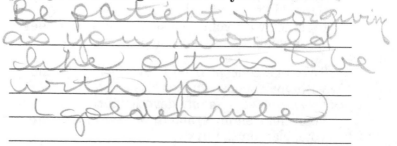

*Be patient + forgivin*
*as you would*
*like others to be*
*with you*
*( golden rule )*

## ACCOUNTABILITY

7. Some important truths about accountability are found in the example of Cain's life recorded in Genesis 4:1-16. Read this passage.

   In verses 6-7, what do you think the Lord was communicating to Cain?

   _If you refuse to obey God, sin is waiting to attack + destroy you_

   How did God deal with Cain's sin? (verses 10-12).

   _God banished him from his land made him a fugitive for life_

8. Look again at Genesis 4:5-12. What were the poor choices Cain made, and how could he have made better choices?

49

| VERSE | CAIN'S CHOICE | A BETTER CHOICE |
|---|---|---|

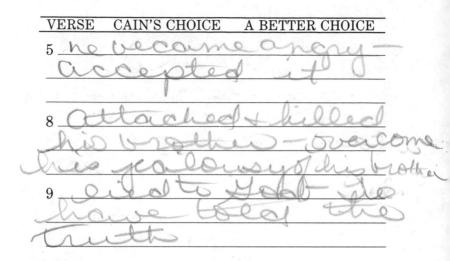

5 *he became angry — accepted it*

8 *attacked + killed his brother — overcome his jealousy of his brother*

9 *lied to God — he have told the truth*

## DEALING WITH TEMPTATION

All of us are often tempted to neglect our God-given responsibilities, and to pursue selfish desires. These temptations, we read in 1 Corinthians 10:13, are "common to man." But temptation can be dealt with and overcome. To adequately carry out their responsibilities throughout life, children must learn the processes for dealing with temptation, asking for and receiving forgiveness, and enjoying victory through Christ.

9. Summarize the process of temptation and sin described in James 1:13-15.

*Temptation is the pull of man's own will thoughts turn she*

50

10. Read 1 Corinthians 10:12-13. List the major principles included in this passage as you would explain them to your children.

*Everyone comes up against temptation. Others have faced them before. You can trust God not to let temptation be more than you can bear.*

11. Read Genesis 3:1-6. What evidence do you see that Eve and Adam were themselves responsible for the sin of eating the forbidden fruit?

*They wanted to become wise. God had told them not to do it.*

12. God has provided a means for cleansing and restoration when we sin. Read 1 John 1:9 and 2:1-2. How do these passages relate to the illustration on the next page?

51

_If we confess our sins to God he can be depended on to forgive us & to cleanse us from every wrong_

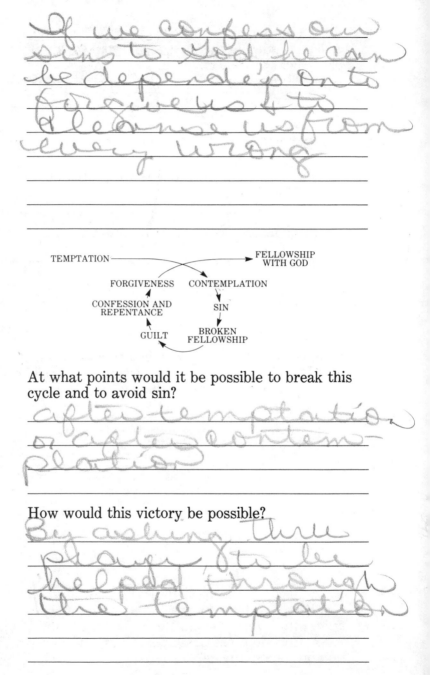

At what points would it be possible to break this cycle and to avoid sin?

_after temptation or after contemplation_

How would this victory be possible?

_By asking thru prayer to be helped through this temptation_

How can we teach this to our children?

*By reading the Bible & teaching them through prayer*

## DEVELOPING
## SELF-CONTROL

Learning to practice self-control is a key area in
developing responsibility.

13. From these passages, list some areas of life in
which we should practice self-control:

Psalm 19:14 *In the things you think & say be pleasing to the Lord*

Proverbs 6:6-11 *work hard, prepare, you will not want*

Proverbs 16:32 *be slow tempered & have self-control*

Philippians 4:8 *think about things that are pure, lovely & dwell on the good things in others, think about all you can be glad about for the*

1 Peter 2:11 *Keep away from evil pleasures of this world*

14. Read Proverbs 25:28. What is a person like who
has no self-control?
*as defenseless as a city with broken-down walls vulnerable to evil*

53

How would you explain the meaning of this verse?

_____

_____

_____

_____

_____

_____

15. Read Galatians 5:22-23 and 2 Timothy 1:7. What resource for self-control do we have?

   *the Holy Spirit*

16. J.B. Phillips* has translated Romans 8:12-13 in this way:

   > "So then, my brothers, you can see that we owe no duty to our sensual nature, or to live life on the level of the instincts. Indeed that way of living leads to certain spiritual death. But if on the other hand you cut the nerve of your instinctive actions by obeying the Spirit, you will live."

   From this passage, what would you say is a key to self-control?

   *obeying the Spirit*

   _____

   _____

   _____

17. What is an area in which you need to practice more self-control?

   *slow tempered + self control*

*The New Testament in Modern English, Revised Edition,* © 1972 by J. B. Phillips (New York: Macmillan).

What steps for improvement can you take this week in this area, so that your life will be an example to your children?

*not to be instantly angered*

Ask God to help you make the correct choices and the right responses each time you fail to exercise self-control. Ask for forgiveness and continue your efforts, remembering that self-control is a fruit of the Holy Spirit (Galatians 5:22-23).

18. What is an area in which you should encourage your children to practice more self-control?

*arguing*

How can you do this?

*Read Bible passage to them*

## APPLICATION

19. Prayerfully review your answers in this chapter. List the things you learned which are most meaningful to you.

*the things we are promised if we obey God, dealing with temptation & learning self-control*

20. Related to what you learned in this chapter, describe any need in your family or your own life that you believe you should work on at this time.

*On self control*

What passage of Scripture in this chapter relates to this need?

*philippians 4:8*

What specific action will you take?

How will you evaluate your progress?

## SUGGESTED FAMILY PROJECT

Make a checkup chart showing various responsibilities in your home or elsewhere for each of your children. Let your children help make the chart, and discuss it with them. Let them suggest changes or additions to the assigned duties, then make sure each one understands the nature of his responsibilities and how often they must be carried out.

## CHAPTER 5

# TRAINING

TRAINING is the day-to-day application of the parental responsibilities God has given us. It is deliberately serving our children to help them lead fulfilled lives in the Lord, being properly prepared to follow the Lord and to face life's challenges. We can guide them confidently, relying on the help of God's Word and His Spirit.

Discipline is a key aspect of this godly training for children.

## DISCIPLINE

> "The term 'discipline' is not limited to the context of punishment. Children also need to be taught *self*-discipline and responsible behavior. They need assistance in learning how to face the challenge and obligations of living. They must learn the art of self-control. They should be equipped with the personal strength needed to meet the demands imposed on them by their school, peer group, and later adult responsibilities."
>
> —James Dobson*

*James Dobson, *Dare to Discipline* (Wheaton, Illinois: Tyndale House, 1970), page 3.

1. Write a paraphrase or summary for each of these passages from Proverbs:

3:11-12 God punishes & corrects you because he loves you so shall parents punish their children because they love them

13:24 If you love your children you will discipline them

22:15 Punish a child when they are rebellious

23:13-14 Do not fail to discipline your children, it wont hurt them punishment will keep them out of hell *learn nothing about being spanked*

29:15 _Scolding & spanking a child helps him to learn. Left to himself, he brings shame to his mother_

29:17 _Discipline your son & he will give you happiness & peace of mind_

What benefits are described in these passages for parents whose children are well-disciplined?

_You will have happiness & peace of mind_

What benefits are described for children when their parents provide proper discipline?

_Helps children to learn, "punishment will keep them out of hell"_ *proverbs 20:18*

2. Read Hebrews 12:9-10. What two sources of discipline are mentioned in this verse?

<u>parents God</u>

How does this passage relate to the discipline you provide for your children?

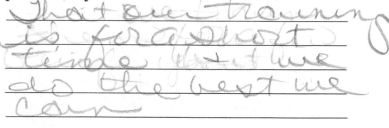

That our training is for a short time, that we do the best we can

3. Describe how Ephesians 6:4 relates to disciplining children:

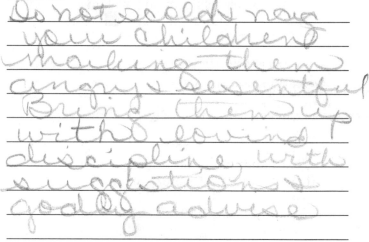

Do not scold nor make your children making them angry & resentful. Bring them up with loving discipline with suggestions & godly advice

4. Discuss with your spouse the principles you have studied in this section regarding discipline. Either before or after your discussion, list the ways in which you think these principles should be practically applied in your family.

*Consistency, communication balanced*

_____

_____

_____

_____

_____

_____

_____

If these principles conflict in any way with how
you discipline your children, how can you change?

_____

_____

_____

_____

_____

_____

_____

_____

_____

## TEACHING

The Book of Proverbs serves as a valuable handbook
for training children. Carefully studying this book
and planning how to implement the principles it
teaches will help you tap its treasures.

One good way to do this is to analyze key
passages from Proverbs (such as those listed on
pages 64-65) to glean out their basic principles, and
to share these with your family.

*p.b.oper*

This can help you think of many possibilities for using the Scriptures, both in planned family times and in spontaneous "teachable" moments in your lives together. Your mind will be primed to take advantage of many opportunities to train your child in Christian living.

You can use the following study questions to help you apply the Scriptures to almost any training situation you encounter with your children.

---

### STUDY QUESTIONS

1. What principles from this passage do I want to teach my children?
2. How should these principles be applied in my family?
3. How can I best put this application into practice? (Here you will need to make specific plans. You may want to teach a principle to the family as a whole, or to one member only. You could try a practical project, a long walk together, a fun activity, setting an example, or some other means of imparting scriptural truth.)
4. When will I do it? (This could be the most crucial aspect of your plan. Decide on a definite time. "Plan your work, then work your plan.")

---

5. Choose a passage and topic appropriate for your family's needs (or for the needs of one individual). You can choose from the list below or use another passage that meets your needs.

   Proverbs 1:32—The need for wisdom
   Proverbs 2:1-6—How to learn
   Proverbs 3:5-6—Trusting in the Lord
   Proverbs 4:1-13—The importance of wisdom
   Proverbs 4:14-19—Avoiding evil
   Proverbs 4:20-27—Guarding your heart and life
   Proverbs 5:1-23—Guarding against adultery

Proverbs 6:6-11—The lesson of the ant
Proverbs 6:16-19—Seven things to avoid
Proverbs 8:1-36—The benefits of wisdom
Proverbs 15:1-4—A controlled tongue
Proverbs 16:1-3—Direction for life
Proverbs 19:5—The results of lying
Proverbs 20:3—The foolishness of quarreling
Proverbs 24:30-34—Recognizing laziness
Proverbs 31:10-31—The noble wife

List your chosen topic and passage here:

*proverbs 41/14-19*

*Avoiding Evil*

6. Read prayerfully through the passage several
times, perhaps using various translations and
paraphrases. After doing this, list here the
number of times you read through the passage.
(You may also want to summarize or paraphrase
this passage here.)

*5*

7. Use a dictionary, a Bible dictionary, or a Bible
encyclopedia to help you learn any words or concepts you do not clearly understand. Record your
findings here.

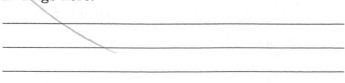

65

8. Read through the following example to see how the four study questions can be used.

---

### HOW TO USE THE FOUR STUDY QUESTIONS

1. What principles from this passage do I want to teach my children?

   Proverbs 2:1-6. This passage deals with proper attitudes toward wisdom. We need to have these attitudes to properly understand and apply the Scriptures—the true source of wisdom. These attitudes include a strong desire to learn, a searching mind and heart, and a willingness to apply what is learned. When we are hungry for truth in this way, we will understand how to know and follow God.

2. How should these principles be applied to my family?

   Anne and Brian need to know clearly how to approach the Word of God in order to benefit the most from its teaching. I need to show them practical ways of taking in the Scriptures, and how I have benefitted from them. I should share with them what I'm learning and applying, and how.

---

3. How can I best put this application into practice?

I will take time to show Anne and Brian what I have been learning in my weekly Bible study, how I make applications, and how God has changed my life in some specific ways through the study: I'm more expressive in my love for them and Joan, have decided to help Brian with his desire to learn more about mechanics, I'm allowing Anne more freedom to visit her friends, and we have all been enjoying the discussions at dinner about scriptural principles I bring up. This could help Anne and Brian in their own Sunday school class to apply the Scriptures they are studying. I will also share with them the verses I've been memorizing.

4. When will I do it?

After Sunday dinner, while we're relaxing at the table.

9. Now use the following study questions with the passage you have chosen. Be sure to write down your thoughts for each question:

67

What principles from this passage do I want to teach my children?

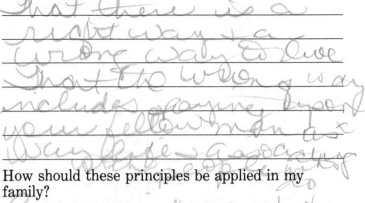

How should these principles be applied in my family?

How can I best put this application into practice?

When will I do it?

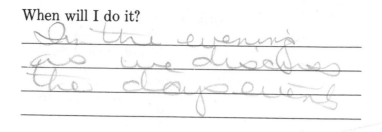

*In the evening as we discuss the day's events*

## FAMILY TIME

One method you may want to use frequently in training your children is having a family time together
centered around a passage of Scripture, or perhaps
other suitable material. Use the study questions on
page 64 to determine the focus of your time, and
follow the guidelines below.

| SUGGESTIONS FOR A GOOD FAMILY TIME |
| --- |

1. Have a plan. Know what you want to share
   or do.
2. Choose times that are convenient for the
   whole family.
3. Have variety. Include both light and serious
   approaches. Here are some possible activities:
   —Reading the Bible
   —Reading Bible story books
   —Reading other Christian books appropriate
     for the family
   —Memorizing and reviewing Scripture
   —Praying
   —Asking questions
   —Acting out Bible stories
   This can also be a good time for just talk-
   ing—sharing with each other the joys and
   victories, as well as the disappointments or
   difficulties in your lives.
4. Include everyone. Let your children plan and
   lead a family time occasionally, based perhaps
   on their Sunday school lesson. Be creative.

5. In a family devotional time, or any time when you and your children are discussing the Bible, it is important for you to talk about the Scriptures on their level. Allow freedom for questions, and treat every question seriously. If you are trying to help them recognize a major truth from the Bible, ask several questions about it from different angles to help you measure their understanding.
6. Keep it simple, short, and relaxed. Your goal in family time is to relate more closely with one another and to help each other learn more about the Christian life.

## CHAPTER 6

# PLANNING FOR THE FUTURE

THROUGH planning we can have a part in shaping the future. Planning is simply deciding ahead of time what we want to do, based on our goals and needs.

A task so important as training our children demands careful evaluation and planning. When this is done in obedience to God and with His guidance, we can anticipate success. "Commit to the Lord whatever you do, and your plans will succeed" (Proverbs 16:3).

## WHY PLAN?

1. What reasons for planning can you find in these passages?

   Psalm 39:4-6 _____

   _____

   _____

   Psalm 90:10,12 _____

   _____

Study the following passage from *The Amplified Bible**
to answer the next four questions. (You may also want
to read the passage in other versions.)

*The Amplified Bible,* © 1965 by Zondervan Publishing House.

"Look carefully then how you walk! Live purpose-
fully and worthily and accurately, not as the unwise
and witless, but as wise, sensible, intelligent people,
making the very most of the time—buying up each
opportunity—because the days are evil. Therefore do
not be vague and thoughtless and foolish, but understanding and firmly grasping what the will of the
Lord is."

—Ephesians 5:15-17

2. How would you describe a person who is unwise in
the use of time?

_____

_____

_____

_____

_____

3. What do you think is involved in living a "purposeful" life?

_____

_____

_____

_____

_____

4. What do you think is the main point of this
passage?

_____

_____

_____

_____

_____

5. How would you describe the relationship between doing God's will and planning?

_____

_____

_____

_____

_____

_____

_____

6. Write out the key thoughts from these passages:

Proverbs 4:25-27 _____

_____

_____

_____

Proverbs 13:16 _____

_____

_____

_____

Proverbs 14:8 _____

_____

_____

_____

7. How do you think the instructions in these passages can be applied to raising a family?

Proverbs 24:3-4 _____

_____

_____

Proverbs 24:27 _____

_____

_____

8. Read Proverbs 21:5. What is the result of good planning?

_____

_____

_____

9. Read Proverbs 12:11. What results from hard work?

_____

_____

_____

10. Summarize what you have learned from this section about planning.

_____

_____

_____

_____

_____

_____

_____

_____

## AN EXERCISE IN PLANNING

The chart on pages 78-79 lists some suggested qualities or activities which could be focal points for training a child at various ages. The list is not comprehensive, but it can stimulate your thinking about how to plan for your children's growth.

Notice that for each broad age range, the topics are divided into four categories: mental, physical, spiritual, and social. These categories correspond to the pattern of Jesus Christ's childhood growth described in Luke 2:52.

Keep these points in mind as you complete this exercise:

• To teach some character quality to your children, you must exhibit the quality yourself. As you observe needs in your children's lives, be sensitive enough to evaluate and improve your own life in these areas.

• Your children may well resist your attempts to teach them unless your goals and plans are motivated by genuine love. They will sense immediately if this love is lacking. Also, if your goals and plans fail, you will be less likely to become frustrated and discouraged if your love for your family is strong.

• Relationships are more important than isolated goals or plans. In the end, it is who you are—the way you actually live your life—that will have a lasting impression on your children, rather than what you try to teach them.

11. For each of your children, list here and on the following page what you now consider to be the most important topics (at least two or three) you should be concerned with in their training for the next six months. Use topics listed in the chart on pages 78-79, or others you think of.

_____

_____

_____

_____

_____

Building these qualities in your children's lives could involve a variety of activities on your part. If you believe your children should develop habits in having personal devotions, more than likely this will mean having a regular devotional time with them, at least for a while. If you believe your child should develop creativity, you may need to help introduce him to outlets for expressing creativity (music or carpentry, for example), being careful to be sensitive to his abilities and interests.

If you selected a topic which is a biblical word or phrase, use a concordance to locate and study the biblical references on the subject. You could then use the suggested guidelines on pages 69-70 to have a family devotional time centered around these passages.

12. From your list in Question 11, select at least one topic for each child, and determine what activities you should pursue to train your children in these areas.

_____

_____

_____

_____

_____

_____

_____

_____

_____

_____

13. How and when will you carry out these activities?

_____

_____

_____

_____

In setting your goals and making plans, remember to make them. . .

specific—not vague.

measurable—Can you look back later and say, "Yes it was done" or "No it wasn't"?

achievable—Can it be done?

realistic—Don't take on too much.

timed—Set a reasonable deadline.

## SELECTED TOPICS FOR TRAINING

| BIRTH TO AGE 6 | AGES 6-12 | AGES 12-20 |
|---|---|---|
| **MENTAL:** | **MENTAL:** | **MENTAL:** |
| Honesty | Determination | Wisdom |
| Speech and other self-expression | Alertness | Discernment |
| Basic reading skills | Appreciation for reading | Financial understanding—budgeting, saving, giving |
| Scripture memory | Scripture memory | Creativity |
| | Good study habits | Initiative |
| | | Decisiveness |
| | | Faithfulness in responsibilities |
| | | Appreciation of nature |
| **PHYSICAL:** | **PHYSICAL:** | **PHYSICAL:** |
| Coordination (as demonstrated by learning to swim, riding a bike, catching a ball, etc.) | Development in hobbies and sports | Endurance |
| Enjoying children's games | Good eating habits | Good habits in physical training |
| Cleanliness and neatness | Learning to work | Confidence in driving a car |
| | Cleanliness and neatness | Controlling sexual appetites |
| | Respecting our bodies as God's temple | Proper knowledge of sex |
| **SPIRITUAL:** | **SPIRITUAL:** | **SPIRITUAL:** |
| Reverence | Self-control | Diligence |
| Obedience and honor to parents | Joyfulness | Love |
| Discipline | Honesty | Faith |
| Forgiveness | Understanding the Gospel | Knowing God's will |
| Faith | Appreciation for devotional time | Confidence in God |
| Truth | | Deeper appreciation for devotional time |
| | | Ability to share the Gospel |
| | | Understanding biblical doctrine |
| | | Overcoming temptation |
| | | Moral purity |
| | | Giving |

| BIRTH TO AGE 6 | AGES 6-12 | AGES 12-20 |
|---|---|---|
| SOCIAL: | SOCIAL: | SOCIAL: |
| Enjoying play with others | Patience | Sincerity |
| Fairness | Dependability | Generosity |
| Attentiveness | Punctuality | Humility |
| Contentment | Loyalty | Relating properly to the opposite sex |
| Gratefulness | Compassion | Courtesy |
| Security | Thoughtfulness | Appearance |
| Meekness | Responsibility | Serving others |
| | Accountability | |

## SUGGESTED FAMILY PROJECT

Using one of the topics you selected for Question 12, plan a family time based on Scripture references on that subject. To prepare, use the study questions introduced in Chapter 5:

What principles from this passage (or passages) do I want to teach my children?

_____

_____

_____

_____

_____

How should these principles be applied to my family?

_____

_____

_____

_____

_____

_____

79

How can I best put these applications into practice?

_____

_____

_____

_____

_____

When will I do it?

_____

_____

_____

## FOR FUTURE PLANNING

Raising children takes many years of effort—and a wise parent will be looking to Scripture continually for guidance and help. The suggestions below can help you in the continuing task of bringing up your children "in the training and instruction of the Lord" (Ephesians 6:4).

a. Extend your Bible study group's work on this topic by repeating the "Exercise in Planning" beginning on page 74, using different topics from the list on pages 78-79. You could do one topic per week for a few more weeks, meeting together regularly to discuss your plans with others in your group. Or, you could repeat the teaching project that begins on page 63, using different passages from the list on pages 64-65 or other passages you choose, and discuss these each week in your group.

b. Use a photocopier to make several copies of the list of study questions on the following page. Use these as a guide for planning frequent times of teaching scriptural principles to your children.

1. What principles from this passage (or passages) do I want to teach my children?

 

 

 

 

 

2. How should these principles be applied in my family?

 

 

 

 

 

3. How can I best put these applications into practice?

 

 

 

 

 

4. When will I do it?

 

 

 

# GUIDELINES FOR GROUP DISCUSSION

Discussing this book in a group—such as a Sunday school class or a Bible study group—will allow greater understanding of the scriptural principles you study. The format for this is simple: The group members first answer the questions to a chapter individually at home, and then discuss their findings with each other when they meet together, which is usually once a week.

If you are the discussion leader for such a group, the material on the following pages will help you guide the group in an edifying time of fellowship centered on God's Word.

## BEFORE THE DISCUSSION

As the group leader, your most important preparation for each session is prayer. You will want to make your prayer requests personal, of course, but here are some suggestions:

• Pray that everyone in the group will complete the chapter preparation, and will attend this week's discussion. Ask God to allow each of them to feel the freedom to honestly share his thoughts, and to make a significant contribution to the discussion.

• Ask God to give each of you new understanding and practical applications from the Scriptures as you talk. Pray that the unique needs of each person will be met in this way.

• Pray that you, as the leader, will know the Holy Spirit's guidance in exercising patience, acceptance, sensitivity, and wisdom. Pray for an atmosphere of genuine love in the group, with each member being honestly open to learning and change.

• Pray that as a result of your study and discussion, all of you will obey the Lord more closely and will more clearly demonstrate Christ's presence in your families.

After prayer, the next most important aspect of your preparation is to be thoroughly familiar with the chapter you're discussing. Make sure you have answered all the questions and have read the leader's material for that chapter.

## GETTING UNDER WAY

When your group is together, work toward having a relaxed and open atmosphere. This may not come quickly, so be especially friendly at first, and communicate to the group that all of you are learning together.

As the leader, take charge in an inoffensive way. The group is looking to you for leadership and you should provide it.

You may want to experiment with various methods for discussing the study material. One simple approach is to discuss it question by question. You can go around the group in order, with the first person giving his answer to Question 1 (followed by a little discussion), the second person answering Question 2, and so on. Or, anyone in the group could answer each question as you come to it (the leader saying something such as "Who would like to take Question 5 for us?"). The question-by-question approach can be a good way to get young Christians started in Bible study discussion. The obvious structure gives them a sense of confidence, and they can see where the discussion is going.

Another method is to lead with a section-by-section

approach. This can provide more spontaneity. Start by asking the group for its impressions of the first section in the chapter you are studying (something like, "What impressed you most from this first section on prayer?"). Remember to direct your question to the entire group, rather than to a certain person.

Someone will then give an answer, probably by referring to a specific question in that section. You can have others share their answers, and then, to discuss the question more thoroughly, ask a thought-provoking question about this topic which you have made up beforehand. Later you'll begin this procedure again with the next section.

The key to a deeper, more interesting and helpful discussion is having good questions prepared. These should challenge the group to look more closely at the subject and Scripture passage you are discussing.

This leader's material includes suggested discussion questions for each chapter in this book. However, you will probably want to write some of your own as well, so make a list before each group meeting. Write as many as you can think of. Having a good supply to choose from will help you quickly launch the discussion, and keep it going in the right direction.

These guidelines will also help:

*Asking questions*

1. Make sure your questions are simple and conversational.
2. Don't be afraid of silence after asking a question. Give everyone time to think.
3. Ask only one question at a time.
4. Don't ask questions which can be answered yes or no. This hinders discussion. Try beginning all your questions with "who," "what," "where," "when," "why," or "how."
5. A "What do you think?" question can help keep the discussion from seeming pressured or unnatural, since there is no such thing as a wrong answer to such a question. The person answering has freedom to simply give his viewpoint.

*Other discussion*
1. Remember that the Scriptures are the source of truth. Often you may want to look up together and read aloud the verses listed for the study questions as you discuss your answers.
2. Summarize frequently. Help the group see the direction of the discussion.
3. Allow time for adequate discussion on the application questions in each chapter. Your goal in Bible study is not, of course, to have something to discuss, but to change your lives.
4. Allow adequate discussion also of the suggested family projects. Talk about how these can be adapted and implemented by everyone in the group.

*General reminders*
1. Your own attitude is a key factor in the group's enthusiasm. Develop a genuine interest in each person's remarks, and expect to learn from them.
2. Concentrate on developing acceptance and concern in the group. Avoid a businesslike atmosphere.
3. Participate in the discussion as a member of the group. Don't be either a lecturer or a silent observer.
4. You may want to begin each session by reviewing memorized Scripture, and then discussing progress made in the previous week on applications and family projects.
5. Your total discussion time should probably not exceed ninety minutes, and one hour might be best. Start and end on time. Remember, too, to close in group prayer.

You'll want to review these lists often.

## AFTER
## THE DISCUSSION

Use these self-evaluation questions after each session to help you improve your leadership the next time:
1. Did you discuss the major points in the chapter?
2. Did you have enough prepared questions to properly guide the discussion?

3. Did you know your material thoroughly enough to have freedom in leading?
4. Did you keep the discussion from wandering?
5. Did everyone participate in the discussion?
6. Was the discussion practical?
7. Did you begin and end on time?

## Chapter 1

## GOALS FOR PARENTS

| OVERVIEW | OBJECTIVE |
|---|---|
| a. Children are a gift from God<br>b. The responsibility of parents<br>c. A promise for parents<br>d. Seeing our children mature<br>e. Application | For parents to understand that child-raising is a God-given privilege and that the father is primarily responsible for his children's spiritual growth; and that if we effectively train our children, God promises to bless our efforts. |

For this session, and in later weeks, you may want to read the chapter objective and overview aloud to the group. This can help them see the overall focus of the chapter as they begin their discussion.

These questions from the study may promote the best discussion in your group as you share with each other your answers to them:

1, 4, 5, 6, 7, 8, 10, 11, and 13.

Each chapter in the study material includes application questions. These are designed to help a person apply a biblical truth to his life in a practical way. Since the written answers for these questions are personal, group members need to have the freedom *not* to share their answers when you are discussing these questions.

87

On the other hand, don't skip over the questions entirely, since the most beneficial discussion you can have is about how the Scriptures affect your day-to-day life.

A good way to stimulate discussion on an application question is to say something like, "Would any of you like to share with us your answers to Question 12?" or, "What did you learn about yourself (or your family) from Question 12?"

(In chapter 1, Questions 12 and 14 are application questions.)

Remember to discuss also the suggested family project. You may want someone to read aloud the instructions. Then discuss how the project can be used and adapted in each family represented in your group.

## FOR FURTHER DISCUSSION

These questions can help you stimulate further discussion on some of the questions in this chapter:

For *Question 1:* How should our relationship with our children be affected by knowing that they are a gift from God?

*Question 4:* How would you summarize the biblical responsibilities given to fathers?

*(Ephesians 6:4):* What do you think it means for a father to "exasperate" his children or to "provoke them to anger"?

*Question 6:* How do the responsibilities of fathers and mothers complement each other?

*Question 7:* How does this passage in Deuteronomy demonstrate God's concern for children?

*Question 10 (1 Timothy 5:8):* How do you think the failure of a Christian to provide for his relatives would be a denial of his faith?

*Question 11:* What confidence can we gain as parents from this passage?

*Question 12:* What are some practical ways we can gauge our children's growth in these areas?

## Chapter 2

# INSTRUCTIONS FOR CHILDREN

| OVERVIEW | OBJECTIVE |
|---|---|
| a. Honoring father and mother<br>b. Helping children learn obedience<br>c. Ingredients for growth<br>d. Application | To understand the importance of instilling within our children a respect for authority—that they learn to honor and obey their parents. |

These questions from the study may promote the best discussion in your group:

1, 5, 7, 8, 9, 10, 13, 14, 15, and 16.

Remember also to discuss the application questions (17 and 18) and the suggested family project.

You may want to have someone read aloud the two paragraphs following Question 14.

At one or two points in the discussion, you may find it appropriate to have a few moments of group prayer about a specific aspect of the study, such as helping our children learn how to obey God, their parents, and other authorities.

## FOR FURTHER DISCUSSION

For *Questions 1-4:* What is your concept of the word *honor?*

*Question 1:* How are *honor* and *obedience* related?

*Question 3:* What evidence do you see that Jesus fully desired to obey His Father?

How can we help our children learn from Jesus' example of obedience?

*Question 5:* What do you think can cause our children to truly want to obey us?

89

What do you think is the main reason they sometimes do not obey us?

This verse (Colossians 3:20) says that the Lord is pleased when children obey their parents. What does this tell us about God's character?

*Questions 8-9:* How important to your children's development is their parents' obedience to God?

*Question 10:* What is the main lesson you see in comparing how God dealt with Eli's sons and how He dealt with Jonadab's sons?

*Question 13:* What to you are the most important things you can pray for your children?

*Question 14:* What do you think are the best ways parents can help children learn the Scriptures?

# Chapter 3

## QUALITIES FOR RIGHT RELATIONSHIPS

| OVERVIEW | OBJECTIVE |
| --- | --- |
| a. Love and acceptance<br>b. Learning from an Old Testament family<br>c. Developing a learner's attitude<br>d. Application | To learn how we can become more loving and accepting of our children, and to help them cultivate a teachable attitude. |

These questions from the study may promote the best discussion in your group:

2, 3, 6, 8, 11, 13, 15, 20, and 21.

The application questions are 4, 12, and 22. Remember also to discuss the suggested family project.

For the section on "Learning from an Old Testament Family" (Questions 6-12), you could launch the discussion by saying, "What did you learn from the example of Isaac's family?"

## FOR FURTHER DISCUSSION

For *Question 3:* How do you think speaking the truth in love helps us mature?

What do you think are the best influences for helping a child learn to always speak the truth?

*Question 5 (1 Thessalonians 2:10-12):* How can a father encourage his children?

How can a father comfort his children?

How can a father urge his children to live lives worthy of God?

*Question 11:* How would you summarize the reasons antagonisms developed between Esau and Jacob?

*Question 12:* What factors are most important in promoting a sense of unity within a family?

*Question 13:* Why do you think the fear of the Lord is such a necessary ingredient for growing in knowledge?

*Question 14-18:* How would you summarize the process in which a person gains wisdom?

*Question 16:* How do you think parents can help their children develop a love for wisdom?

*Question 18:* What do you think are the best sources for children to get advice and instruction?

## Chapter 4

## TEACHING RESPONSIBILITY

| OVERVIEW | OBJECTIVE |
|---|---|
| a. Sowing and reaping<br>b. Accountability<br>c. Dealing with temptation<br>d. Developing self-control<br>e. Application | To become better equipped to help our children develop responsibility—becoming willingly accountable for their words and actions. |

These questions may promote the best discussion in your group:

2, 3, 7, 8, 10, 12, 14, 16, and 19.

Questions 5, 17, 18, and 20 are application questions.

## FOR FURTHER DISCUSSION

For *Question 1:* In your own experience, how have you observed the principle of sowing and reaping as it is described in Galatians 6:7-9?

*Question 3:* How do you think Jesus' teaching in Luke 16:10-12 should be applied to raising children?

*Question 7:* What do you think prompted Cain to commit his sin?

*Question 9:* How can a child be taught to recognize the process of temptation and sin?

*Question 12:* What should be the relationship between God's forgiveness of your child for something he has done wrong, and your own forgiveness of the child?

*Question 14:* How have you observed that a child is harmed by lacking self-control?

*Questions 15-16:* How can you communicate to a child the importance of living by God's Spirit?

## Chapter 5

## TRAINING

| OVERVIEW | OBJECTIVE |
| --- | --- |
| a. Discipline<br>b. Teaching<br>c. Family time | To become familiar with biblical principles on discipline so as to apply them in our families, and to gain practice in thinking how to train our children. |

Allow plenty of time to discuss Question 9, which is an application question, after your discussion of Questions 1-4.

You may want to have various group members read aloud all the material in the "Family Time" section, and then discuss it.

## FOR FURTHER DISCUSSION

For *Questions 1-4:* How would you define proper discipline?

*Question 2:* How is God's discipline an example for us in disciplining our children?

*Questions 5-9:* What is the relationship between discipline and teaching?

## Chapter 6

## PLANNING FOR THE FUTURE

| OVERVIEW | OBJECTIVE |
|---|---|
| a. Why plan?<br>b. An exercise in<br>   planning<br>c. For future planning | To understand the value of planning, and to gain practice in planning for our children's future. |

Allow plenty of time to discuss your answers to Questions 11-13, as well as the suggested family project and the section entitled "For Future Planning."

## FOR FURTHER DISCUSSION

For *Question 1 (Psalm 39:4-6):* When you think about how uncertain the length of your life is, how does it affect your thinking about planning for the future?

93

*(Psalm 90:12):* How do we gain a "heart of wisdom"?

*Question 2:* What are some practical ways we can evaluate our use of time?

*Question 3:* What for you is a truly purposeful life?

*Question 6 (Proverbs 4:25-27):* What do you think it means for us to keep our eyes looking straight ahead?

*Questions 8-9:* What is the relationship between good planning and hard work?

# SUGGESTED READING

Campbell, Donald K. *How to Really Love Your Child.*
Wheaton, Illinois: Victor Books, 1977.

Dobson, James. *Dare to Discipline.* Wheaton, Illinois:
Tyndale House, 1970.

MacDonald, Gordon. *The Effective Father.*
Philadelphia: Westminster Press, 1977.

Murray, Andrew. *How to Raise Your Children for
Christ.* Minneapolis: Bethany Fellowship, 1976.

Narramore, Bruce. *Help! I'm a Parent.* Grand
Rapids, Michigan: Zondervan Publishing House,
1972.

Shedd, Charlie W. *Letters to Karen.* Old Tappan,
New Jersey: Fleming H. Revell, 1965.

———. *Letters to Philip.* Old Tappan, New Jersey:
Fleming H. Revell, 1969.

Matthew 18:3 come like
a little child